MW00862011

Journal to

A Fun Homeschooling History Curriculum for Kids!

Ancient Civilizations of the World: Mesopotamia, Egypt, Greece, and Rome

By

The Insightful Scholar

Part of The Insightful Scholar History Curriculum Series

MAAC Publishing
Written and Published in the USA
ISBN 979-8-9870786-5-5

theinsightfulscholar.com
info@theinsightfulscholar.com

About This Book

The scope of the reading book and workbook focus on Mesopotamia and the Mediterranean regions due to the volume of information covered. However, we explore other ancient civilizations around the world in other books.

This Journal follows the same topics and all three books are intended to complement each other. Students can also use the internet, library books, and videos to assist in their research.

We provide several valuable free resources to supplement this curriculum, which you can access at theinsightfulscholar.com.

These resources include:

- Parent-Teacher Guide (includes answers to workbook questions)
- Bibliography with additional references
- Color images with citations
- Glossary
- Timeline

Introduction

Come On Explorers, Let's Go!

_____

_____

_____

_____

_____

_____

_____

_____

_____

_____

_____

_____

_____

_____

_____

_____

_____

It's Doodle Time!

Let's Get Creative!

We ♥ Art!

Those are some Wild Wonders!

Chapter 1
Becoming Civilized

It's Doodle Time!

Let's Get Creative!

We  Art!

Chapter 2
The Sumerians

How Many "Firsts" Can You Name?

It's Doodle Time!

Let's Get Creative!

We ♥ Art!

How Many Languages Can You Speak?

Chapter 3
The Babylonians

It's Doodle Time!

Let's Get Creative!

We 🖤 Art!

Chapter 4
Egyptian Civilizations

What's Another Word For Emoji? Logogram!

Hapi   Duamutef   Qebehsenuef   Imsety

It's Doodle Time!

Let's Get Creative!

We  Art!

Chapter 5
Egyptian Time Periods

It's Doodle Time!

Let's Get Creative!

We ♥ Art!

Chapter 6
Other Mediterranean

Tyrian Purple
Is Our
Favorite Color!

’
B
G
D
H
W
Z
Ḥ

Ṭ
Y
K
L
M
N
S
‘

P
Ṣ
Q
R
Š
T

It's Doodle Time!

Let's Get Creative!

We 💛 Art!

What Is Your Favorite Olympic Sport?

Chapter 7
The Greeks

It's Doodle Time!

Let's Get Creative!

We  Art!

Chapter 8
The Romans

It's Toga Time!

It's Doodle Time!

Let's Get Creative!

We 🖤 Art!

Conclusion

(speech bubble: What A Great Adventure Explorers!)

It's Doodle Time!

Let's Get Creative!

We ♥ Art!

Made in the USA
Las Vegas, NV
10 May 2024

89767189R10070